Healthy
Kitchen™

D0186688

Veggie
& vegan

Imprint

Seven

Produced by Seven Publishing on behalf of WW International, Inc. Published May 2019.

Seven Publishing Ltd,
3-7 Herbal Hill, London EC1R 5EJ
www.seven.co.uk

A CIP catalogue record for this book is available from the British Library.

ISBN: 978-1-9996673-5-1

WW PUBLISHING TEAM
Samantha Rees, Harriet Joy, Ruby Bamford, Nicola Kirk

FOR SEVEN PUBLISHING LTD
FOOD
Food editor: Nadine Brown
Recipes: Nadine Brown, Ella Tarn

EDITORIAL
Editor-in-Chief: Helen Renshaw
Editor: Ward Hellewell
Sub-editors: Christine Faughlin, Sarah Allen, Sarah Nittinger

DESIGN & PHOTOGRAPHY
Art director: Liz Baird
Photographer: Tom Regester
Food stylists: Amber De Florio, Ella Tarn
Prop stylist: Agathe Gits

ACCOUNT MANAGEMENT
Account manager: Gina Cavaciuti
Group publishing director: Kirsten Price

PRODUCTION
Senior production manager: Liz Knipe
Colour reproduction by F1 Colour
Printed in the UK by CPI Colour

THE SMALL PRINT

Eggs We use medium eggs, unless otherwise stated. Pregnant women, the elderly and children should avoid recipes with eggs which are raw or not fully cooked if not produced under the British Lion code of practice.

Fruit and vegetables Recipes use medium-size fruit and veg, unless otherwise stated.

Reduced-fat soft cheese Where a recipe uses reduced-fat soft cheese, we mean a soft cheese with 30% less fat than its full-fat equivalent.

Low-fat spread When a recipe uses a low-fat spread, we mean a spread with a fat content of no more than 39%.

Microwaves If we have used a microwave in any of our recipes, the timings will be for an 850-watt microwave oven.

Prep and cook times These are approximate and meant to be guidelines only. Prep time includes all steps up to and following the main cooking time(s). Stated cook times may vary according to your oven.

Vegetarian Recipes displaying a vegetarian symbol include non-meat ingredients, but may also contain processed products that aren't always vegetarian, such as pesto. If you're a vegetarian, you should ensure you use vegetarian varieties and check the ingredients labels. Where we reference vegetarian Italian-style hard cheese in vegetarian recipes, we mean a cheese similar to Parmesan (which is not vegetarian) but which is suitable for vegetarians.

Vegan Recipes displaying a vegan symbol include no products made from or with the aid of animals or animal products.

Gluten free Recipes that are labelled as gluten free include ingredients that naturally do not contain gluten, but they may also contain processed products, such as sauces, stock cubes and spice mixes. If so, you should ensure that those products do not include any gluten-containing ingredients (wheat, barley or rye) – these will be highlighted in the ingredients list on the product label. Manufacturers may also indicate whether there is a chance their product may have been accidentally contaminated with gluten during the manufacturing process. For more information and guidance on gluten-free products, visit www.coeliac.org.uk

Nut free Recipes displaying a nut free symbol include ingredients that do not contain nuts, but may include ingredients produced in facilities that also handle nut products. If you have a nut allergy, check ingredients labels for more information.

Dairy free Recipes displaying a dairy free symbol include ingredients that naturally do not contain dairy, but may include ingredients produced in facilities that also handle dairy products. If you have a dairy allergy, check ingredients labels for more information.

SmartPoints® have been calculated using the values for generic foods, not brands (except where stated). Tracking using branded items may affect the recorded SmartPoints.

When you see these symbols:

0   **Tells you the SmartPoints value per serving**

    Indicates a recipe is vegan

    Indicates a recipe is gluten free

    Indicates a recipe is nut free

    Indicates a recipe is vegetarian

    Indicates a recipe is dairy free

Contents

8   **Introduction**

10   **Vegan swaps**

11   **Top tips**

12   **Breakfast**

34   **Lunch**

62   **Dinner**

90   **Snacks & desserts**

112   **Index**

Colourful, varied and delicious

– vegetables take centre stage in this book, which is packed with easy-to-achieve ideas that will soon become your go-to recipes. Whether you're vegetarian, vegan or would like to switch up your meal plan with a few meat-free dishes, you'll find plenty of recipes inside that are simple and satisfying. We've come up with some tasty plant-based twists on your favourite meals, such as our amazing vegan fry-up (p16), Caprese-style panini with vegan 'mozzarella' (p46) and sweet and sour cauliflower (p78) – our delicious Chinese fakeaway. There are also plenty of ideas for snacks and desserts to keep you on track.

Smart swaps for vegan cooking

Choosing to eat a vegan diet doesn't mean you have to miss out on dishes you love. All it takes are a few clever tweaks to make your meals vegan-friendly.

INSTEAD OF CHEESE...
use nutritional yeast
With its nutty, cheesy flavour, nutritional yeast makes a great addition to sauces and it's perfect for sprinkling on top of pasta and other dishes that call for grated cheese. It's also a way to get extra vitamin B12, which may otherwise be in short supply in a vegan diet. Sometimes sold as 'yeast flakes', you can find it in health food stores and some supermarkets.
TRY: Butternut mac & 'cheese', p86

INSTEAD OF MILK...
use nut, oat or soya milk
There are plenty of of alternatives to cow's milk, and most are easily available. Nut milks can be made from almonds, hazelnuts or cashews, and can have a noticeable flavour, while soya and oat milk have a more neutral taste. Use them as you would cow's milk – in your tea or coffee and other drinks, to make sauces, or in baking recipes. Make sure you buy unsweetened versions.
TRY: Cherry Bakewell Bircher muesli, p20

INSTEAD OF BUTTER...
use dairy-free spread
Plant-based spreads can be used in most recipes that call for butter, but check the labels as some are not vegan and may contain milk or other dairy products. Dairy-free spreads will work just as well as butter in vegan bakes, and can also be used to make buttercream-style frostings and fillings.
TRY: Chocolate celebration cake, p110

INSTEAD OF YOGURT...
use soya yogurt
You can swap regular cow's milk yogurt for plain soya yogurt in most recipes. Soya yogurt is made from soya milk and yogurt cultures, and it may also have a small amount of added sugar to help the fermentation process.
TRY: Roasted broccoli houmous with crudités, p94

INSTEAD OF GELATINE...
use agar agar
Agar agar is made from a type of algae, but don't let that put you off – it doesn't have a distinct taste, but will still help desserts firm up. It comes in powder or flake form and has to be boiled in liquid before it will set. It sets slightly firmer than gelatine, and will stay set at higher temperatures.

INSTEAD OF MEAT... use jackfruit
A tropical fruit that's native to south Asia, jackfruit has a firm texture similar to shredded meat. You can find it fresh in the UK, but the best option to use as a meat substitute is the variety that's tinned in brine or water (available in most big supermarkets). It's made from green fruit, rather than riper fruit which has a higher sugar content.
TRY: Pulled jackfruit burgers, p88

INSTEAD OF SCRAMBLED EGGS...
use tofu
When crumbled and fried with herbs and seasoning, tofu resembles scrambled egg in taste and texture – a great replacement for regular hen's eggs.
TRY: Herby scrambled tofu with grilled tomatoes, p30

INSTEAD OF EGG WHITES...
use chickpea water
Also known as aquafaba, the liquid drained from tinned chickpeas contains starches and proteins that make it a useful substitute for eggs in recipes such as meringue. You will need to beat it for a bit longer than regular egg white to reach the right consistency, but with a little patience, you'll be rewarded with great results.
TRY: Lemon meringue tart, p106

INSTEAD OF HONEY...
use agave or maple syrup
For a hint of sweetness in recipes that call for honey, try agave or maple syrup instead. Maple syrup has a distinctive smoky flavour, while agave has a more neutral taste, so you can use whichever suits the recipe best. Both maple and agave syrups are 1 SmartPoint per teaspoon.
TRY: Summer rolls, p100

Veggie-licious!

Veggie and vegan meals can be just as flavourful and interesting (if not more so!) as recipes that contain meat. Here are 10 top tips for adding extra taste and texture.

Perfect match

Experiment with flavour combinations by pairing ingredients that naturally work well together. A good rule of thumb is to balance spicy, salty, bitter, sweet and sour flavours, so that no one flavour is too dominant.
TRY: Beetroot & feta galette, p82

Spice things up

Dried spices and fresh herbs are a quick way to add a lot of flavour for no extra SmartPoints. Black peppercorns, smoked paprika, and curry powder are all good staples to have to hand. As a rule, it's best to add fresh herbs at the end of the cooking time so they don't lose their flavour or colour.
Try: Smoky aubergine chilli, p72

Dial up the flavour

Strong flavours like ginger, wasabi or sesame oil pack plenty of taste into a dish and you won't need much to make an impact. Sun-dried tomatoes and olives are also good options, especially in pasta dishes.
TRY: Sun-dried tomato carbonara, p74

In with the new

Try something new – don't get stuck in a rut trying to find substitutes for meat. Instead, celebrate veg! Build your meals around an interesting vegetable, or adapt your favourite recipes to use veg in place of meat.
Try: Lentil & okra curry, p84

Best bites

Texture is just as important as flavour in creating delicious veggie dishes. Mushrooms, aubergines and jackfruit all have a meaty texture that help keep things interesting.
Try: Griddled aubergine bánh mì, p36

In a pickle

Use a quick pickling technique to transform raw vegetables – it doesn't take long, but is a great way to add crunch and lots of fresh zingy flavour to salads and sandwiches. Carrots, cucumbers, radishes and onions are all great for pickling.
TRY: Roasted chickpea gyros, p58

Crunch time

Toss toasted nuts and seeds into salads, use breadcrumbs to coat tofu or meat alternatives, or roast veg and pulses to add lots of extra crunch to meals.
TRY: Tofu nuggets, p98

Get ready to roast

Roasting, griddling or barbecuing veg enhances its natural taste, caramelises the natural sugars in the vegetables and often adds a delicious smoky flavour.
TRY: Tahini butternut couscous bowl, p48

The heat is on

Before you use nuts, seeds or whole spices in your recipes, try toasting them in a dry frying pan – it'll enhance the flavour of your dish and only takes an extra minute or two. Take care that they don't burn – as soon as they become fragrant, they're done.
TRY: Kale, mango & cashew salad, p42

Season to taste

Veg benefits from plenty of seasoning, so use salt and freshly ground black pepper to taste, or finish off with a squeeze of lemon or lime juice to really make the flavours sing. Remember to taste the food before serving, and adjust the seasoning if you need to.

Breakfast

14   Butter bean pancakes with fresh strawberries

16   Vegan fry-up

18   Moroccan-style avocado on toast

20   Cherry Bakewell Bircher muesli

22   Breakfast burrito

24   Oat waffles with mixed berries

26   Menemen

28   Hash brown traybake

30   Herby scrambled tofu with griddled tomatoes

32   Apricot & pistachio breakfast bars

Butter bean pancakes with fresh strawberries

serves 4   **prep time** 15 minutes + resting   **cook time** 20 minutes   **freezable**

Added beans helps keep the SmartPoints low, and the pancakes are just as delicious.

400g tin butter beans, drained and rinsed
2 eggs
2 tablespoons clear honey
2 teaspoons vanilla extract
150g self-raising flour, sifted
150ml skimmed milk
Calorie controlled cooking spray
200g 0% fat natural Greek yogurt
200g strawberries, hulled and diced

1   Put the beans and 4 tablespoons water in a food processor and blitz until completely smooth. Add the eggs, 1 tablespoon of the honey and the vanilla extract, and blitz again until completely combined. Transfer the mixture to a large bowl and add the flour. Gradually add the milk, whisking, until you have a smooth batter. Cover and set aside for 15 minutes.

2   Mist a large nonstick frying pan with cooking spray and set over a medium-high heat. Once hot, ladle in 4 scoops of batter to make 4 pancakes about 8-9cm in diameter. Cook for 2-3 minutes or until bubbles start to appear on the surface. Flip and cook for another 1 minute or until golden. Transfer to a plate and keep warm. Repeat with the remaining batter to make 12 pancakes in total.

3   Combine the yogurt with ½ tablespoon of the honey in a small bowl. To serve, stack 3 pancakes per person and top with the yogurt, diced strawberries and the remaining honey.

The pancakes can be frozen in an airtight container for up to 2 months.

 SmartPoints value per serving

Vegan fry-up

serves 4   prep time 20 minutes   cook time 1 hour 10 minutes

Fancy a fry up? This vegan version includes crisp, delicious carrot 'bacon'.

Calorie controlled cooking spray

400g button mushrooms, halved

1 tablespoon finely chopped fresh flat-leaf parsley

4 large tomatoes, halved

4 slices WW Thick Wholemeal Bread, toasted, to serve

FOR THE 'BACON'

1 tablespoon olive oil

1½ tablespoons vegan Worcestershire sauce

½ tablespoon maple syrup

½ tablespoon dark soy sauce

½ tablespoon sweet smoked paprika

4 carrots, peeled into thin strips using a vegetable peeler

FOR THE BEANS

1 small onion, finely chopped

2 garlic cloves, finely chopped

1 teaspoon ground cumin

1 tablespoon sweet smoked paprika

2 x 400g tins cherry tomatoes

400g tin haricot beans, drained and rinsed

1 Preheat the oven to 140°C, fan 120°C, gas mark 1 and line 2 large baking trays with baking paper.

2 Toss all of the 'bacon' ingredients together in a mixing bowl, then arrange the carrot strips in a single layer on the prepared baking trays, reserving the marinade. Bake for 1 hour to 1 hour 10 minutes, basting with the reserved marinade halfway through, until the carrots are crisp. Set aside.

3 Meanwhile, make the beans. Mist a large nonstick frying pan with cooking spray and set over a medium-high heat. Add the onion and cook for 6-8 minutes, until soft. Add the garlic and spices and cook for another minute, then stir in the tomatoes and simmer for 15 minutes. Add the beans and simmer for a further 5 minutes.

4 Mist a large nonstick frying pan with cooking spray and fry the mushrooms over a medium-high heat for 3-4 minutes. Stir through the parsley, then push the mushrooms to one side of the pan. Add the fresh tomatoes, cut side-down, and cook for 2 minutes, then turn over and cook for another minute.

5 Top the toast with the beans and serve with the mushrooms, tomatoes and 'bacon'.

 SmartPoints value per serving

Cook's tip

Add 1 frozen Quorn Cumberland vegan sausage, cooked to pack instructions for 3 extra SmartPoints per serving.

Moroccan-style avocado on toast

serves 4   prep time 5 minutes   cook time 5 minutes

Spice up your smashed avo on toast with this quick and easy vegan recipe.

1½ avocados, peeled and stone removed (235g prepared weight)
Juice of ½ lemon
1 garlic clove, crushed
4 x 30g slices sourdough bread
2 teaspoons pomegranate seeds
1 teaspoon ras el hanout

1   Cut ¾ of the whole avocado into 12 slices. Put the remaining avocado in a small bowl with the lemon juice and garlic, and mash with a fork. Season to taste.

2   Toast the bread, then spread with the mashed avocado and top with the avocado slices. Scatter over the pomegranate seeds and serve sprinkled with the ras el hanout.

6 **SmartPoints value per serving**

Cherry Bakewell Bircher muesli

serves 4   prep time 10 minutes + overnight chilling   cook time 5 minutes

These delicious overnight oats are topped with juicy cherries and crunchy almonds.

140g porridge oats
1 small apple, cored and grated
1 tablespoon chia seeds
550ml unsweetened almond milk
**1 tablespoon agave syrup, plus
1 teaspoon extra for the compote**
3-4 drops almond extract
250g frozen cherries, thawed
Grated zest of ½ orange
**4 teaspoons toasted
flaked almonds**

1   Put the oats, apple and chia seeds in a large bowl and stir to combine. Add the almond milk, 1 tablespoon of the agave syrup and the almond extract and stir until combined. Cover and put in the fridge to chill overnight.

2   Before you're ready to serve, make the compote. Put the cherries, orange zest and remaining agave syrup in a medium pan. Bring to a boil, then reduce the heat and simmer for a few minutes until the cherries are softened and just heated through. Drain off and discard 1 tablespoon of the liquid, then roughly crush the cherries with a fork, keeping some of them whole.

3   Divide the oat mixture between bowls, then serve topped with the cherry compote and the flaked almonds.

  SmartPoints value per serving

Cook's tip
A dollop of plain soya yogurt
will add creaminess without
any additional SmartPoints.

Breakfast burrito

makes 4   prep time 15 minutes   cook time 20 minutes

This is perfect if you fancy adding a Mexican twist to your breakfast.

Calorie controlled cooking spray
1 small red onion, finely diced
1 small red pepper, deseeded and diced
1 green chilli, deseeded and finely diced
½ teaspoon ground cumin
½ teaspoon smoked paprika
4 eggs
4 WW White Wraps
1 avocado, peeled, stone removed and diced (155g prepared weight)
400g tin borlotti beans, drained and rinsed
60g half-fat Cheddar, grated
2 tablespoons chopped fresh coriander
Tabasco sauce, to serve
Lime wedges, to serve

1   Mist a large nonstick frying pan with cooking spray and set over a medium heat. Add the onion, pepper and chilli and cook for 6-8 minutes until the onion and pepper are soft. Add the cumin and paprika and cook for another 1-2 minutes.

2   Whisk the eggs in a mixing bowl with 1 tablespoon of water. Reduce the heat to low and add the eggs to the pan. Cook for about 5-7 minutes, folding the mixture with a silicone spatula, until the eggs are just barely set. Season to taste.

3   Heat the wraps in the microwave to pack instructions. Lay the wraps on a work surface and top with the eggs, followed by the avocado, beans and cheese. Season to taste, then scatter over some of the coriander and a few drops of Tabasco.

4   Tuck in the ends of the wraps and roll each one up, then serve with the lime wedges on the side.

 7 **SmartPoints value per burrito**

Oat waffles with mixed berries

serves 2   prep time 10 minutes + standing   cook time 10 minutes

These oaty vegan waffles are crisp, fluffy and delicious.

125ml oat milk

75g porridge oats

3 small ripe bananas, roughly chopped (you'll need 250g)

4 tablespoons plain soya yogurt

200g strawberries, hulled and quartered

150g raspberries

150g blueberries

2 teaspoons maple syrup

1 Put the oat milk, oats and bananas in a food processor and blitz until you have a smooth batter. Leave to stand for 20 minutes – the mixture should be thick, but pourable.

2 Preheat a waffle maker according to its settings. Pour in the batter, being careful not to overfill – this mixture is enough to make 2 square waffles. Cook according to your waffle maker instructions until the waffles are cooked through and golden.

3 Serve the waffles topped with the yogurt and berries, with the maple syrup drizzled over.

 SmartPoints value per serving

Cook's tip

You can also make these in a silicone mould. Bake at 200°C, fan 180°C, gas mark 6 for 10-12 minutes or until set.

Menemen

serves 4   prep time 10 minutes   cook time 25 minutes

This Turkish dish of spicy scrambled eggs and veg is great at any time of the day.

2 tablespoons olive oil

1 teaspoon smoked paprika

½ teaspoon dried oregano

¼ teaspoon dried mint

1 small onion, finely diced

1 green pepper, deseeded and finely diced

3 tomatoes, diced

6 eggs, lightly beaten

2 tablespoons chopped fresh flat-leaf parsley

4 slices WW Soft Malted Danish Bread

1   Put the oil in a nonstick frying pan and set over a low heat until warm, but not hot. Add the paprika, oregano, mint, onion and green pepper, and season to taste. Cook, stirring often, for 8-10 minutes until the vegetables are soft.

2   Add the tomatoes and continue to cook, stirring often, for 6-8 minutes until the tomatoes start to break down and the mixture becomes darker in colour. Remove half of the mixture and set aside.

3   Add the eggs to the pan and season to taste. Cook for about 5-7 minutes, folding the mixture with a silicone spatula, until the eggs are just barely set.

4   Remove from the heat, gently fold in the reserved vegetable mixture and garnish with the parsley. Toast the bread and serve with the eggs.

  SmartPoints value per serving

Cook's tip

This delicious breakfast dish is a staple in Turkey. It should be cooked gently over a low heat to ensure soft, velvety eggs.

Hash brown traybake

serves 6   prep time 20 minutes   cook time 35 minutes

This easy veggie traybake is perfect for a weekend family breakfast.

600g potatoes, coarsely grated
250g carrots, coarsely grated
500g courgettes, trimmed and coarsely grated
7 eggs
120g half-fat Cheddar, coarsely grated
2 tablespoons plain flour
2 tablespoons snipped fresh chives, plus extra to serve
Calorie controlled cooking spray
400g button mushrooms, halved
400g tin baked beans

1 Preheat the oven to 200°C, fan 180°C, gas mark 6. Pile the grated veg onto the centre of a large square of muslin or clean tea towel, squeeze out any excess liquid, then put the veg into a large bowl. Lightly beat 1 of the eggs and add it to the bowl along with 75g of the cheese, and the flour and chives. Season to taste and stir to combine.

2 Mist a 20cm x 30cm baking tray with cooking spray, then add the hash brown mixture and spread out into an even layer. Scatter over the remaining cheese and mist with cooking spray. Bake for 30-35 minutes, or until crisp and golden.

3 Meanwhile, mist a nonstick frying pan with cooking spray and set over a medium-high heat. Add the mushrooms and cook for 3-4 minutes, or until golden, then transfer to a bowl and set aside. Wipe the pan clean, then mist with more cooking spray and fry the remaining eggs for 2 minutes, until the whites are set and the yolks soft.

4 While the eggs are cooking, warm the beans in a small pan set over a low heat.

5 Cut the hash brown into 6 pieces and serve topped with the fried eggs and a sprinkling of freshly ground black pepper and chives, with the mushrooms and beans on the side.

Cook's tip
Use 250g grated butternut squash in place of the carrots for the same SmartPoints.

6 **SmartPoints value per serving**

Herby scrambled tofu with griddled tomatoes

serves 4   prep time 10 minutes   cook time 10 minutes

This vegan alternative to scrambled eggs is a tasty way to start the day.

300g cherry tomatoes on the vine

1 tablespoon olive oil

2 x 396g packs extra-firm tofu

2 garlic cloves, crushed

½ teaspoon ground turmeric

2 tablespoons chopped fresh flat-leaf parsley, plus extra to serve

2 tablespoons snipped fresh chives, plus extra to serve

4 bagel thins

1   Set a nonstick griddle pan over a medium heat. Brush the tomatoes with a little of the oil and season to taste. When the pan is hot, add the tomatoes and cook for 4-5 minutes until tender and blistered.

2   Meanwhile, drain the tofu and gently squeeze out any excess liquid. Crumble the tofu into a bowl so you have even-size pieces without any large chunks.

3   Add the remaining oil to a large nonstick frying pan and set over a medium heat. Add the garlic and cook for 1 minute until fragrant, then add the tofu and cook, stirring gently, for 3-4 minutes.

4   Sprinkle the turmeric over the tofu, then cook for a further 2-3 minutes, stirring gently, until the tofu is yellow throughout. Remove from the heat and stir through the fresh herbs, then season to taste.

5   Toast the bagel thins and serve topped with the scrambled tofu and the grilled tomatoes, with the extra fresh herbs scattered over.

5   SmartPoints value per serving

Apricot & pistachio breakfast bars

makes 16   prep time 5 minutes + cooling   cook time 35 minutes   freezable

Try one of these tasty oat-based bars for an on-the-go breakfast or afternoon snack.

100g pistachio kernels

250g oats

½ teaspoon ground ginger

½ teaspoon ground cinnamon, plus extra to serve

80g dried apricots, roughly chopped

2 large ripe bananas, mashed (you'll need 300g)

100g maple syrup

30g ball stem ginger, finely chopped

1   Preheat the oven to 180°C, fan 160°C, gas mark 4 and line a 26cm x 16cm baking tin with baking paper.

2   Put the pistachio kernels onto a separate baking tray and bake for 8-10 minutes, or until golden. Roughly chop, then put into a mixing bowl.

3   Add all of the remaining ingredients to the bowl and stir to combine. Press the mixture into the prepared baking tin, using the back of the spoon to level it and making sure it reaches into the corners. Bake for 20-25 minutes, or until just golden, then set aside to cool completely in the tin.

4   Lift the baked oat mixture (on the baking paper) from the tin, scatter over the extra cinnamon, and cut into 16 bars.

Store the bars in a freezer bag and freeze for up to 1 month, or keep in the fridge in an airtight container for up to five days.

5   **SmartPoints value per breakfast bar**

Cook's tip

When lining the baking tin, leave some of the baking paper hanging over the edge, then use it to lift the baked bars out of the tin once they're cooked.

Lunch

36   Griddled aubergine bánh mì

38   Bombay potato frittata

40   Primavera orzo pasta salad

42   Kale, mango & cashew salad

44   Green goddess egg muffins

46   Caprese panini rolls

48   Tahini butternut couscous bowl

50   Beetroot falafel pittas

52   Smoky borlotti bean soup

54   Coronation chickpea open sandwich

56   Veggie sushi bowl

58   Roasted chickpea gyros

60   Moroccan-style cauliflower soup

Griddled aubergine bánh mì

makes 4 **prep time 10 minutes** **cook time 25 minutes**

This popular Vietnamese street food packs flavoursome fillings into fresh baguettes.

2 large aubergines, trimmed and cut into 5mm-thick slices

1 garlic clove, crushed

Calorie controlled cooking spray

70g red cabbage, finely shredded

1 large carrot, peeled into ribbons with a vegetable peeler

1 tablespoon rapeseed oil

½ tablespoon rice vinegar (see Cook's tip)

2 teaspoons agave syrup

Juice of ½ lime

½ red chilli, deseeded and finely chopped

4 x 70g white baguettes

Small handful fresh mint leaves

1 Set a large nonstick griddle pan over a medium-high heat. Rub the aubergine slices with the garlic, then mist with cooking spray. Season to taste. When the griddle is smoking hot, add the aubergine slices and cook for 3 minutes on each side, until tender and charred, then transfer to a plate and set aside. You will need to do this in batches.

2 Put the cabbage and carrot into a small bowl. In a small jug, whisk together the oil, vinegar, agave syrup, lime juice and chilli. Add the dressing to the cabbage and carrot, then toss together and set aside.

3 Split the baguettes lengthways. Layer with the aubergine, cabbage, carrot and mint, then serve.

7 **SmartPoints value per bánh mì**

Cook's tip
Use regular white wine vinegar if you don't have any rice vinegar.

Bombay potato frittata

serves 4   prep time 10 minutes + cooling   cook time 35 minutes

A spicy Indian twist on a simple frittata, this goes perfectly with a salad for lunch.

800g potatoes, diced

Calorie controlled cooking spray

1 large onion, thinly sliced

2 tablespoons mild curry paste

500g large tomatoes, halved, deseeded and roughly chopped

8 large eggs, lightly beaten

2 tablespoons chopped fresh coriander

Mixed salad leaves, to serve

1   Cook the potatoes in a pan of boiling water for 12-15 minutes until just tender, then drain and set aside.

2   Meanwhile, mist a deep nonstick ovenproof pan with cooking spray and set over a medium heat. Add the sliced onion and cook for 6-8 minutes, until soft. Stir in the curry paste and continue to cook for another minute, then add the tomatoes and cook for a further minute. Add the cooked potatoes, stir to combine, then season to taste.

3   Preheat the oven to 200°C, fan 180°C, gas mark 6. Pour the beaten eggs over the potato mixture, then cook on the hob for 7-8 minutes, or until the eggs have just started to set. Transfer the pan to the oven and bake for 10 minutes, or until the frittata is completely set.

4   Remove the pan from the oven and set aside to cool for 5 minutes. Scatter over the fresh coriander, then cut into wedges and serve with the salad on the side.

 SmartPoints value per serving

Cook's tip

Beat eggs very lightly when making a frittata. Overbeating will cause it to rise in the oven, then sink into a dense layer.

Primavera orzo pasta salad

serves 4   prep time 10 minutes   cook time 10 minutes

An easy lunchtime pasta salad that's packed with green veg and fresh herbs.

300g orzo pasta

200g asparagus, trimmed and cut into 4cm lengths

200g Tenderstem broccoli, cut into 4cm pieces

100g frozen peas

1 leek, trimmed and finely sliced

150g half-fat crème fraîche

30g reduced-fat green pesto

Pared zest of 1 lemon, plus ½ tablespoon lemon juice

Small handful fresh flat-leaf parsley, roughly chopped, plus extra to serve

Small handful fresh mint, finely chopped, plus extra whole leaves to serve

Lemon wedges, to serve

1   In a large pan of boiling water, cook the orzo to pack instructions, adding the asparagus, broccoli, peas and leek for the final 4 minutes of cooking time. Drain, refresh under cold running water, then drain again. Set aside.

2   In a small bowl, combine the crème fraîche, pesto and lemon juice, then set aside.

3   In a large serving bowl, toss together the orzo and vegetables with the crème fraîche dressing and most of the lemon zest. Season to taste, then stir in the herbs.

4   Top with with the extra parsley and mint leaves and the remaining lemon zest, then serve with the lemon wedges on the side.

 SmartPoints value per serving

Cook's tip

To make vegan pesto, blitz 20g basil, 1½ tablespoons pine nuts, 2 garlic cloves and 2 tablespoons nutritional yeast in a small food processor until a paste forms. With the machine running, drizzle in 1 tablespoon olive oil. Gradually add 60ml water until the pesto is your desired consistency. This makes 8 tablespoons at 1 SmartPoint per tablespoon, and will not affect the SmartPoints in the above recipe.

Kale, mango & cashew salad

serves 4   prep time 10 minutes   cook time 10 minutes

Chilli and mango add spice and fruity flavour to this colourful salad.

75g unsalted cashew nuts
1 tablespoon olive oil
3 tablespoons lemon juice
250g shredded kale
200g red cabbage, shredded
150g plain soya yogurt
1 teaspoon agave syrup
½ teaspoon ground turmeric
1 large garlic clove,
finely chopped
1 large mango, peeled, stone
removed and sliced
1 small red chilli, deseeded
and finely chopped

1   Preheat the oven to 180°C, fan 160°C, gas mark 4. Put the cashew nuts on a small baking tray and roast for 10 minutes until lightly golden and fragrant. Set aside to cool completely.

2   Meanwhile, in a small bowl, combine the olive oil and 1 tablespoon of the lemon juice. Put the kale and cabbage in a large serving bowl and drizzle over the olive oil and lemon juice mixture. Massage gently with your hands until the kale starts to soften.

3   Put the soya yogurt, agave syrup, turmeric and garlic in a small bowl with the remaining lemon juice, season to taste and whisk until combined.

4   Toss the mango slices, red chilli and toasted cashew nuts through the kale salad, then serve drizzled with the dressing.

5   **SmartPoints value per serving**

Cook's tip
Massaging the kale helps to
break down the tough fibres,
making it easier to eat.

Green goddess egg muffins

serves 4   prep time 10 minutes + cooling   cook time 25 minutes

These egg muffins, packed with broccoli and asparagus, make a simple, tasty lunch.

½ tablespoon olive oil

150g asparagus, trimmed and cut into 3cm lengths

100g Tenderstem broccoli, cut into 3cm pieces

8 large eggs, lightly beaten

80g half-fat crème fraîche

1 tablespoon finely chopped fresh tarragon

2 tablespoons finely chopped fresh flat-leaf parsley

1 tablespoon snipped fresh chives

FOR THE SALAD

10 cherry tomatoes, halved

100g mixed salad leaves

½ cucumber, peeled into ribbons with a vegetable peeler

2 x 20g sachets WW Classic Garlic & Chive dressing

1   Preheat the oven to 190°C, fan 170°C, gas mark 5. Using a pastry brush, grease a 12-hole muffin tin with the oil. Transfer the tin to the oven to heat.

2   Cook the asparagus and broccoli in a pan of boiling water for 3 minutes, or until just tender. Drain, refresh under cold running water and drain again. Set aside.

3   Put the eggs and crème fraîche into a large jug, season to taste, and whisk until frothy. Stir in the fresh herbs, then carefully pour the mixture into the prepared tin. Top with the broccoli and asparagus, then bake for 15-20 minutes, until set and golden.

4   Set aside to cool completely in the tin, then gently release the muffins by running a knife around the edges.

5   Put the tomatoes, salad leaves and cucumber in a serving bowl, pour over the dressing and gently toss to combine. Serve 3 muffins per person with the salad on the side.

2   SmartPoints value per serving

Cook's tip

The muffins will keep in the fridge for up to a week and are great for popping in a lunchbox or for picnics.

Caprese panini rolls

makes 4   prep time 15 minutes + cooling & chilling   cook time 15 minutes

Enjoy these cafe-style toasted rolls filled with tomatoes and vegan 'mozzarella'.

3 tablespoons vegan mayonnaise
4 x 85g panini rolls, split
4 large tomatoes, sliced
Small handful fresh basil leaves
Calorie controlled cooking spray

FOR THE VEGAN 'MOZZARELLA'
250g firm tofu
250ml unsweetened almond milk
3½ tablespoons cornflour
10g nutritional yeast
1 teaspoon lemon juice

1   To make the vegan 'mozzarella', put the tofu, almond milk, cornflour, nutritional yeast and lemon juice into a blender and blitz until smooth. Transfer the mixture to a small pan set over a medium heat and cook for 8-10 minutes, whisking constantly, until thick. Pour the mixture into two ramekins and allow to cool, then put in the fridge to chill for 1 hour 30 minutes, or until set.

2   Carefully turn the 'mozzarella' out of the ramekins and cut into 5mm-thick rounds. Set aside.

3   Spread the mayonnaise over the cut sides of the panini rolls, then top the bases with the tomatoes, basil leaves and 'mozzarella'. Season to taste, then add the tops of the rolls and mist all over with cooking spray.

4   Set a large griddle pan over a medium-high heat, then add the panini rolls (you may need to do this in batches) and cook for 2-3 minutes on each side, pressing down with a spatula, until the 'mozzarella' is melting and the rolls are golden. Serve immediately.

12   SmartPoints value per roll

Cook's tip
You can store the 'mozzarella' in a bowl of salted water in the fridge for 3-4 days.

Tahini butternut couscous bowl

serves 4   prep time 15 minutes   cook time 45 minutes

This colourful bowl includes roasted veg and a delicious tahini dressing.

1 butternut squash (about 1.2kg), peeled, deseeded and cut into wedges

2 red onions, cut into wedges

3 garlic cloves, unpeeled

Calorie controlled cooking spray

200g wholewheat giant couscous

1½ tablespoons tahini

Grated zest and juice of ½ lemon

½ tablespoon agave syrup

Small handful fresh dill, chopped

Small handful fresh flat-leaf parsley, chopped

3 chargrilled peppers in brine, drained and sliced

50g sun-dried tomatoes

1   Preheat the oven to 200°C, fan 180°C, gas mark 6. Put the butternut squash, onions and garlic into a roasting tin and mist with cooking spray. Season to taste and roast for 20 minutes, then remove the garlic and turn the vegetables over. Return to the oven and roast for another 15-20 minutes until the vegetables are tender and golden.

2   Meanwhile, cook the couscous to pack instructions and set aside. Put the tahini, lemon juice and agave syrup into a mini blender or food processor with 2 tablespoons cold water. Squeeze the roasted garlic cloves from their skins into the food processor, then blitz until smooth. Set aside.

3   Toss the couscous with most of the herbs and divide between bowls. Top with the roasted butternut squash and onions, followed by the peppers and sun-dried tomatoes. Drizzle over the tahini dressing and scatter over the lemon zest and extra herbs, then serve.

 8   **SmartPoints value per serving**

Cook's tip
You could serve this with some crusty white bread – a 50g slice will add 4 SmartPoints per serving.

Beetroot falafel pittas

makes 4   **prep time 15 minutes**   **cook time 35 minutes**

Adding beetroot to these chickpea falafels gives them extra flavour and colour.

250g cooked beetroot (not in vinegar), roughly chopped

400g tin chickpeas, drained and rinsed

4 tablespoons plain flour

1 teaspoon ground cumin

1 teaspoon ground coriander

1 garlic clove, crushed

2 tablespoons chopped fresh coriander, plus extra to serve

Calorie controlled cooking spray

1 tablespoon sesame seeds

½ cucumber, trimmed, halved lengthways, seeds removed and sliced

120g fat-free natural yogurt

2 tablespoons finely chopped fresh mint, plus extra leaves, to serve

4 wholemeal pitta breads

6 tablespoons reduced-fat houmous

60g mixed salad leaves

1   Preheat the oven to 200°C, fan 180°C, gas mark 6 and line a baking tray with baking paper.

2   Put the beetroot, chickpeas, flour, spices, garlic and fresh coriander into a food processor. Season to taste, then blitz to a coarse paste. Form the mixture into 12 balls and put on the prepared tray. Press each ball to flatten slightly, then mist with cooking spray and scatter over the sesame seeds. Bake for 30-35 minutes until crisp on the outside.

3   Combine the cucumber, yogurt and mint in a small bowl. Split the pittas and fill with the houmous and falafels. Top with the salad, minted cucumber yogurt and extra mint leaves, then cut in half and serve.

   SmartPoints value per pitta

Cook's tip
To make this vegan, use plain soya yogurt for no extra SmartPoints.

Smoky borlotti bean soup

serves 4   prep time 5 minutes   cook time 40 minutes   freezable

This tasty vegan soup is great for batch cooking and freezing for later.

Calorie controlled cooking spray
1 small onion, finely chopped
1 celery stick, finely chopped
2 garlic cloves, crushed
2 fresh bay leaves
1 tablespoon sweet smoked paprika, plus extra to serve
400g tin chopped tomatoes
500ml vegetable stock, made with 1 stock cube
2 x 400g tins borlotti beans, drained and rinsed
100g Savoy cabbage, shredded
100g plain soya yogurt

1 Mist a large pan with cooking spray and set over a medium heat. Add the onion and celery and cook for 8-10 minutes until soft. Add the garlic, bay leaves and paprika, and cook for another minute, then stir in the tomatoes and stock. Cover and bring to a boil, then reduce the heat and simmer for 20 minutes. Add the beans, stir to combine, and simmer for another 5 minutes.

2 Remove the bay leaves, then use a stick blender to blitz the soup until it's mostly smooth, but with some of the beans left whole.

3 Season to taste, then stir in the cabbage and cook for another 2-3 minutes or until the cabbage is tender.

4 Ladle the soup into bowls and serve garnished with a swirl of the yogurt and the extra paprika.

The soup can be frozen in an airtight container for up to 2 months.

0 **SmartPoints value per serving**

Cook's tip
You could serve this with some crusty bread – a 50g slice of sourdough will add 4 SmartPoints per serving.

Coronation chickpea open sandwich

makes 4   prep time 5 minutes   cook time 2 minutes

A quick and easy lunch that will keep you full until dinner.

2 tablespoons mango chutney

150g 0% fat natural Greek yogurt

2 teaspoons mild curry powder

**Juice of ½ lemon, plus
lemon wedges to serve**

**2 x 400g tins chickpeas, drained
and rinsed**

**1 tablespoon finely chopped fresh
coriander, plus extra to serve**

25g sultanas

4 x 40g slices sourdough bread

40g rocket

1   Put the chutney, yogurt, curry powder and lemon juice into a large bowl and stir to combine. Add the chickpeas, coriander and sultanas, season to taste, and stir to combine.

2   Toast the bread, then top each slice with the rocket followed by the chickpea mixture. Garnish with the extra coriander, then season to taste and serve with lemon wedges on the side.

   SmartPoints value per sandwich

Veggie sushi bowl

serves 4   prep time 10 minutes + pickling   cook time 35 minutes

A Japanese-inspired rice bowl with pickled veg and a wasabi dressing.

250g sushi rice

2 large carrots, peeled into ribbons with a vegetable peeler

1 large cucumber, peeled into ribbons with a vegetable peeler

3½ tablespoons rice wine vinegar

½ tablespoon agave syrup

1 tablespoon thinly sliced fresh ginger

1 teaspoon black sesame seeds

1 tablespoon sesame oil

2 tablespoons soy sauce

¼ teaspoon wasabi paste

1 red pepper, deseeded and thinly sliced

175g ready-cooked edamame beans

20g pickled ginger

1 Rinse and drain the rice, then cook to pack instructions.

2 Meanwhile, put the carrots and cucumber in a small bowl and pour over 3 tablespoons of the vinegar and the agave syrup. Add the fresh ginger and set aside to pickle for 10 minutes, then drain and toss with the sesame seeds. Remove and discard the ginger.

3 Combine the sesame oil, soy sauce, wasabi paste and remaining vinegar in a small bowl and set aside.

4 Divide the rice between bowls and top with the pickled vegetables, red pepper, edamame beans and pickled ginger, then drizzle over the wasabi dressing and serve.

8 SmartPoints value per serving

Cook's tip
Use white sesame seeds if you can't find black ones.

Roasted chickpea gyros

makes 4   prep time 10 minutes + cooling   cook time 35 minutes

Soft, Greek-style flatbreads filled with spicy chickpeas and salad.

**2 x 400g tin chickpeas, drained
and rinsed**

**1 tablespoon sweet
smoked paprika**

1 teaspoon ground cumin

1 teaspoon ground coriander

½ tablespoon olive oil

4 tablespoons red wine vinegar

2 teaspoons caster sugar

1 small red onion, thinly sliced

**½ cucumber, trimmed, halved
lengthways, then deseeded and
thinly sliced**

200g fat-free natural yogurt

**2 tablespoons finely chopped
fresh mint**

4 x 65g folded flatbreads

40g mixed salad leaves

1   Preheat the oven to 200°C, fan 180°C, gas mark 6. Spread
    the chickpeas out on a baking tray and pat dry with kitchen
    paper. Transfer to a large bowl, add the spices and oil and toss
    together to coat. Season to taste, then return to the baking tray.
    Bake for 30-35 minutes, stirring halfway, until crisp.

2   Meanwhile, put the vinegar and sugar in a small pan set over a
    low heat and cook, stirring, for 5 minutes, or until the sugar has
    dissolved. Transfer to a small bowl, add the onion, and toss to
    combine. Set aside for 30 minutes to cool and for the onion to
    pickle, then drain.

3   Put the cucumber, yogurt and mint into a bowl, season to taste
    and gently toss to combine.

4   Fill each flatbread with the cucumber and yogurt mixture,
    roasted chickpeas, pickled onions and salad leaves, then serve.

 SmartPoints value per gyros

Moroccan-style cauliflower soup

serves 4   prep time 10 minutes   cook time 30 minutes

A fragrant, lightly spiced soup that's a real showstopper.

Calorie controlled cooking spray
1 small onion, finely chopped
2 garlic cloves, crushed
1½ teaspoons ground cumin
½ teaspoon ground cinnamon
½ teaspoon ground coriander
2 tablespoons harissa paste
1 litre hot vegetable stock, made with 2 stock cubes
1 large cauliflower, cut into florets
40g blanched almonds
150g 0% fat natural Greek yogurt

1   Mist a large nonstick pan with cooking spray and set over a medium heat. Add the onion and cook for 6-8 minutes, until soft. Add the garlic, spices and 1½ tablespoons of the harissa paste and cook for another minute.

2   Stir in the stock and cauliflower florets and simmer for 20 minutes, or until the cauliflower is tender. Season to taste and remove from the heat. Using a stick blender, blitz the cauliflower mixture until smooth. Set aside and keep warm.

3   Meanwhile, toast the almonds in a small dry frying pan set over a low heat until just golden, then allow to cool slightly and roughly chop. In a small bowl, combine the remaining harissa paste and the yogurt, then set aside.

4   Serve the soup with the harissa and yogurt mixture swirled through and the toasted almonds scattered over the top.

3 SmartPoints value per serving

Dinner

64   Olive & artichoke tart

66   Halloumi curry

68   Romesco-style pasta bake

70   Sweetcorn & carrot fritters

72   Smoky aubergine chilli with cauliflower 'rice'

74   Sun-dried tomato carbonara

76   Cheese & onion pie with minted greens

78   Sweet & sour cauliflower with rice

80   Green tagine with preserved lemon couscous

82   Beetroot & feta filo galette

84   Lentil & okra curry

86   Butternut squash mac & 'cheese'

88   Pulled jackfruit burgers with celeriac fries

Olive & artichoke tart

serves 6   prep time 20 minutes + chilling   cook time 50 minutes

This Mediterranean-style tart is delicious served with a simple side salad.

½ tablespoon plain flour, for dusting

375g sheet ready-rolled light shortcrust pastry (215g used)

4 large eggs, lightly beaten

100g half-fat crème fraîche

25g vegetarian Italian-style hard cheese, grated

2 tablespoons finely chopped fresh flat-leaf parsley, plus extra to serve

2 tablespoons finely chopped fresh dill, plus extra to serve

400g tin artichoke hearts in water, drained and sliced

100g pitted green olives in brine, drained and halved

Mixed salad leaves, to serve

1 Preheat the oven to 190°C, fan 170°C, gas mark 5. Lightly dust a work surface with the flour, unroll the pastry, then use a rolling pin to further roll it out to a circle that's 25cm in diameter and 3mm thick.

2 Line a 20cm fluted loose-bottomed tart tin with the pastry, then trim and discard the excess. Prick the pastry all over with a fork, then transfer to the fridge and chill for 20 minutes.

3 Line the chilled pastry case with baking paper and fill with baking beans. Blind bake for 15 minutes, then remove the beans and bake for a further 5-10 minutes, until just golden.

4 Meanwhile, put the eggs, crème fraîche, 4 tablespoons of the cheese and all of the herbs into a medium bowl and whisk to combine. Season to taste. Scatter the artichoke hearts and olives over the base of the baked pastry case, then pour over the egg mixture. Scatter over the remaining cheese, then bake for 20-25 minutes, or until the filling is set and golden.

5 Set aside to cool slightly, then scatter over the extra parsley and dill. Cut the tart into wedges and serve with the salad leaves.

 SmartPoints value per serving

Cook's tip

This tart is also great served cold as part of a lunch buffet. You can use black olives, instead of green, if you prefer.

Halloumi curry

serves 4   prep time 10 minutes   cook time 35 minutes   freezable

Firm-textured halloumi works really well in this simple veggie curry.

Calorie controlled cooking spray

1 large onion, finely sliced

2 garlic cloves, finely chopped

½ red chilli, deseeded and finely chopped

1½ tablespoons mild curry powder

400g tin chopped tomatoes

300ml vegetable stock, made with 1 stock cube

200g green beans, trimmed

250g light halloumi, cut into 3cm cubes

400g tin chickpeas, drained and rinsed

2 x 250g pouches microwave brown basmati rice

100g fat-free natural yogurt

Small handful fresh coriander leaves, to serve

Lime wedges, to serve

1   Mist a large nonstick pan with cooking spray and set over a medium heat. Add the onion and cook for 6-8 minutes, until soft. Stir in the garlic, chilli and curry powder, and cook for another minute. Stir in the tomatoes and stock, then bring to a simmer and cook for 15 minutes. Remove from the heat.

2   Meanwhile, cook the green beans in a pan of boiling water until just tender, then drain and set aside.

3   Meanwhile, mist a nonstick frying pan with cooking spray and set over a high heat. Add the halloumi and cook for 2-3 minutes, stirring, until golden. Gently stir the halloumi, chickpeas and green beans into the curry, then return the pan to a low heat and cook for 6-8 minutes until the chickpeas are warmed through and the beans are tender. Season to taste.

4   Prepare the rice to pack instructions, then divide between bowls. Top with the curry and yogurt and serve garnished with the coriander, with the lime wedges on the side.

The curry will keep in an airtight container in the fridge for up to 2 days, or in the freezer for up to 1 month.

12   **SmartPoints value per serving**

Cook's tip

To make this recipe vegan, leave out the halloumi and add 250g extra-firm tofu, cut into 3cm cubes, and serve with a dairy-free yogurt. The SmartPoints will be 6 per serving.

Romesco-style pasta bake

serves 4   prep time 10 minutes + cooling   cook time 50 minutes   freezable

Who doesn't love a pasta bake? This one has a red pepper sauce with a spicy kick.

4 red peppers

600g cherry tomatoes

300g fusilli pasta

½ tablespoon olive oil

2 small garlic cloves, crushed

2 teaspoons chilli flakes, plus extra to serve

Small handful fresh basil, roughly torn, plus extra to serve

125g light mozzarella, torn

1 Heat the grill to high. Prick the skin of the peppers and tomatoes all over with a small knife, then arrange on a large baking tray. Grill, turning occasionally, for 20-25 minutes until soft and slightly charred. Transfer to a heatproof bowl, cover with clingfilm and set aside to cool for 10 minutes. When the peppers are cool enough to handle, peel and discard the skin, seeds and stem. Slice one of the peppers and set aside.

2 While the vegetables are grilling, cook the pasta for 8-10 minutes until just al dente, then drain, return to the pan and set aside.

3 Put the 3 whole peppers and all of the grilled tomatoes into a food processor. Add the oil, garlic, chilli flakes and torn basil, season to taste and blitz until smooth. Preheat the oven to 200°C, fan 180°C, gas mark 6.

4 Add the pepper and tomato sauce to the pan with the pasta and stir to combine. Put half the mixture in a 22cm x 22cm deep baking dish, then top with half of the mozzarella and half of the sliced pepper. Layer the remaining pasta, mozzarella and sliced pepper, then bake for 20-25 minutes, until the cheese is melted and the sauce is bubbling. Serve topped with the extra basil and chilli flakes.

The pasta bake can be frozen for up to 1 month, unbaked and wrapped in foil in the baking dish. Defrost overnight in the fridge, then bake as in step 4.

Cook's tip

Make sure to check the mozzarella packaging, as not all brands are vegetarian.

10 **SmartPoints value per serving**

Sweetcorn & carrot fritters

serves 4   prep time 20 minutes   cook time 25 minutes

Crisp veggie fritters are served with a soft fried egg and chickpea salad.

2 x 198g tins sweetcorn, drained

2 large carrots, coarsely grated (you'll need about 150g)

1 small garlic clove, crushed

1 teaspoon ground cumin

2 teaspoons smoked paprika

80g self-raising flour

5 eggs

Calorie controlled cooking spray

100g fat-free natural yogurt

Juice of 1 lemon

2 x 400g tins chickpeas, drained and rinsed

400g cherry tomatoes, quartered

1 small red onion, finely sliced

Small handful fresh flat-leaf parsley, finely chopped, plus extra to serve

1   Preheat the oven to 160°C, fan 140°C, gas mark 3. Put the sweetcorn, carrots, garlic and spices into a bowl and stir to combine. Season to taste, then stir in the flour. Beat 1 of the eggs, then add to the mixture and mix well. Form the mixture into 8 patties, then transfer to a plate and set aside.

2   Mist a large nonstick frying pan with cooking spray and set over a medium-high heat. Fry the patties in batches of 4 for 3 minutes on each side, until just golden. Transfer to a baking sheet and keep warm in the oven, then repeat with the remaining patties.

3   Wipe the pan clean, then mist with more cooking spray and fry the remaining eggs for 3-4 minutes, or until the whites are set and the yolks are still soft.

4   Meanwhile, combine the yogurt and lemon juice in a small bowl, then season to taste. In a separate bowl, toss together the chickpeas, tomatoes and red onion, then spoon over the yogurt mixture. Scatter over the parsley and toss to combine.

5   Serve the fritters with the fried eggs and chickpea salad, with the extra parsley and some freshly ground black pepper scattered over.

 SmartPoints value per serving

Smoky aubergine chilli with cauliflower 'rice'

serves 4   **prep time 5 minutes**   **cook time 35 minutes**   **freezable**

A mild, fragrant curry of tender aubergines, tomatoes and kidney beans.

Calorie controlled cooking spray
1 small red onion, finely chopped
2 garlic cloves, finely chopped
1 tablespoon tomato purée
½ tablespoon ground cumin
½ teaspoon mild chilli powder
1 tablespoon sweet smoked paprika, plus extra to serve
½ tablespoon dried oregano
2 large aubergines, cut into 1½cm pieces
400g tin chopped tomatoes
400ml vegetable stock, made with 1 stock cube
400g tin kidney beans, drained and rinsed
Grated zest and juice of ½ lime, plus lime wedges, to serve
500g cauliflower 'rice'
100g plain soya yogurt, to serve
Small handful fresh coriander leaves, to serve

1   Mist a large nonstick pan with cooking spray and set over a medium-high heat. Add the onion and cook for 6-8 minutes until soft. Add the garlic, tomato purée, spices and dried oregano, and cook for another 2 minutes.

2   Stir in the aubergines and cook for 1 minute, then add the chopped tomatoes and stock. Stir to combine then bring to a boil. Reduce the heat and simmer uncovered for 20 minutes, until the aubergine is tender.

3   Add the kidney beans and the lime juice, then season to taste. Simmer for another 5 minutes, until the beans are warmed through.

4   Meanwhile, mist a large nonstick frying pan with cooking spray and set over a medium heat. Add the cauliflower 'rice' and cook, stirring, for 5 minutes until tender.

5   Put the yogurt in a small bowl and sprinkle over the lime zest and extra paprika. Serve the chilli with the cauliflower 'rice', yogurt and lime wedges, with the coriander scattered over the top.

The chilli can be frozen in an airtight container for up to 2 months.

1   **SmartPoints value per serving**

Cook's tip
Try serving the chilli with 30g tortilla chips per person, for an extra 4 SmartPoints per serving.

Sun-dried tomato carbonara

serves 4   prep time 5 minutes   cook time 15 minutes

Sun-dried tomatoes add a delicious flavour to this traditional pasta dish.

300g linguine

3 tablespoons dairy-free spread

2 garlic cloves, crushed

3 tablespoons plain flour

600ml unsweetened almond milk

30g nutritional yeast

100g sun-dried tomatoes in oil, drained and sliced

2 tablespoons finely chopped fresh flat-leaf parsley, plus extra to serve

1   Cook the pasta to pack instructions, then drain and set aside.

2   Meanwhile, set a large nonstick pan over a medium-high heat and add the spread. When melted, add the garlic and cook for 1 minute. Stir in the flour and cook for another 2 minutes, then gradually whisk in the almond milk until smooth and combined. Stir in the nutritional yeast, then bring to a simmer and cook for 8-10 minutes, until the sauce has thickened. Season to taste.

3   Add the cooked pasta to the pan and toss to coat in the sauce. Stir in the sun-dried tomatoes and parsley, then serve garnished with the extra parsley and some freshly ground black pepper.

 SmartPoints value per serving

Cook's tip
Serve this with 5g grated vegan hard cheese scattered over per serving for 1 extra SmartPoint.

Cheese & onion pie with minted greens

serves 4   prep time 15 minutes   cook time 50 minutes

This hearty vegetarian pie is perfect for a weekend family dinner.

400g potatoes, cut into 3cm pieces

Calorie controlled cooking spray

2 large onions, finely chopped

2 garlic cloves, crushed

200g half-fat mature Cheddar, coarsely grated

2 tablespoons finely chopped fresh flat-leaf parsley

3 large eggs, lightly beaten

320g ready-rolled light puff pastry (160g used)

200g Tenderstem broccoli

200g frozen peas, thawed

1 tablespoon low-fat spread

1 tablespoon finely chopped fresh mint

1 Cook the potatoes in a large pan of boiling water for 10-15 minutes until just tender, then drain and allow to steam dry in the sieve or colander.

2 Meanwhile, mist a large nonstick frying pan with cooking spray and set over a medium heat. Add the onions and cook for 15 minutes until soft and starting to caramelise. Add the garlic and cook for another minute, then transfer to a large bowl. Add the cooked potatoes, cheese and parsley. Reserve 1 tablespoon of the beaten eggs, then add the rest to the bowl. Season to taste and gently stir to combine.

3 Preheat the oven to 200°C, fan 180°C, gas mark 6. Put the cheese and onion mixture into a 24cm shallow pie dish. Unroll the pastry and place it over the top of the filling, then trim off and discard the excess. Crimp the edges of the pastry, cut a small slit into the top of the pie to allow steam to escape, then brush the pastry all over with the reserved egg. Bake for 30-35 minutes until the pastry is puffed and golden.

4 While the pie is baking, cook the broccoli in a pan of boiling water for 3 minutes, then add the peas and cook for another minute. Drain, return the veg to the pan and add the spread and mint. Stir until the spread has melted.

5 Serve the pie seasoned with freshly ground black pepper, with the veg on the side.

 **12 SmartPoints value per serving**

Sweet & sour cauliflower with rice

serves 4   prep time 10 minutes   cook time 25 minutes

This vegan version of the Chinese takeaway favourite is packed with colour and flavour.

1 large cauliflower, broken into florets

1 small onion, cut into wedges

1 red and 1 green pepper, both deseeded and cut into 3cm strips

2 garlic cloves, thickly sliced

½ tablespoon vegetable oil

2 tablespoons light soy sauce

2 tablespoons cornflour

60g reduced-sugar tomato ketchup

½ x 435g tin pineapple chunks in juice, drained and juice reserved (you'll need approximately 150ml)

3 tablespoons rice vinegar

2 x 250g pouches microwave basmati rice

2 spring onions, trimmed and finely sliced, to serve

1 Preheat the oven to 200°C, fan 180°C, gas mark 6. Put the cauliflower, onion, peppers, and garlic on a large baking tray, drizzle over the oil and toss to coat. Roast for 20 minutes, or until the veg is tender.

2 Meanwhile, combine the soy sauce and cornflour in a small bowl. Put the mixture in a nonstick wok or frying pan set over a medium heat, then whisk in the ketchup, pineapple juice, vinegar and 350ml water. Simmer the mixture for 4-5 minutes until thickened, then add the roasted vegetables and the pineapple. Cook, stirring, for 1 minute until everything is coated in the sauce.

3 Prepare the rice to pack instructions, then divide between bowls. Top with the sweet and sour cauliflower. Serve garnished with the spring onions.

 SmartPoints value per serving

Cook's tip
Try serving this dish with 1 tablespoon black sesame seeds scattered over the top, for an extra 1 SmartPoint per serving.

Green tagine with preserved lemon couscous

serves 4   prep time 10 minutes   cook time 20 minutes   freezable

A delicious Moroccan-style dish that features a medley of green veg and herbs.

Calorie controlled cooking spray

1 large onion, thinly sliced

1 large fennel bulb, trimmed, cored and thinly sliced, fronds reserved

2 garlic cloves, finely chopped

1 teaspoon ground ginger

1 teaspoon ground coriander

1 cinnamon stick

350ml vegetable stock, made with 1 stock cube

4 courgettes, trimmed and cut into 4cm chunks

100g pitted green olives in brine, drained and halved

2 tablespoons chopped fresh flat-leaf parsley, plus extra to serve

2 tablespoons chopped fresh coriander, plus extra to serve

200g couscous

2 preserved lemons in brine, drained, halved and finely chopped

Juice of ½ lemon

1   Mist a large flameproof casserole or tagine dish with cooking spray and set over a medium heat. Add the onion and fennel and cook, covered, for 10-12 minutes until soft, then stir in the garlic and all of the spices and cook for another minute. Stir in the stock, courgettes and olives and simmer for 5 minutes. Remove and discard the cinnamon stick. Season to taste, then stir in the fresh herbs.

2   Meanwhile, put the couscous and preserved lemons in a large bowl and pour over 250ml boiling water from the kettle. Cover with clingfilm, then set aside for 5 minutes, until all the liquid has been absorbed. Fluff up the grains with a fork, then stir through the lemon juice and season to taste.

3   Serve the lemon couscous topped with the tagine and garnished with the extra parsley and coriander, and the reserved fennel fronds.

The tagine can be frozen in an airtight container for up to 2 months.

6   **SmartPoints value per serving**

Cook's tip

If you can't find preserved lemons, you can use the finely grated zest of 1 lemon instead. The SmartPoints will remain the same.

Beetroot & feta filo galette

serves 4   prep time 15 minutes   cook time 20 minutes

Sweet beetroot, earthy lentils and salty feta combine perfectly in this simple tart.

250g cooked beetroot (not in vinegar), cut into thin wedges

½ x 250g pouch cooked Puy lentils

3 sprigs fresh thyme, leaves picked

1 teaspoon dried oregano

½ tablespoon balsamic vinegar

100g light feta, crumbled

4 sheets filo pastry, halved widthways

1 tablespoon olive oil

1 tablespoon chopped fresh flat-leaf parsley, to serve

1   Preheat the oven to 190°C, fan 170°C, gas mark 5. Put the beetroot, lentils, thyme, dried oregano and balsamic vinegar in a bowl and season to taste. Toss everything together, then scatter over half the feta and fold gently to combine.

2   Line a baking tray with baking paper and top with one piece of the filo pastry. Lightly brush the pastry with the oil, then top with a second piece of pastry at a slight angle to the first. Brush with oil, then repeat with the remaining pastry and oil.

3   Pile the beetroot mixture into the centre of the pastry, leaving a 5-6cm border. Fold the border over the filling and brush the pastry edges with any remaining oil. Bake for 15-20 minutes until the pastry is crisp and golden.

4   Scatter over the remaining feta and parsley, then serve.

 SmartPoints value per serving

Cook's tip

This is delicious served with a simple green salad. For a vegan version, use vegan Greek-style cheese for an extra 2 SmartPoints per serving. Most filo pastry is vegan, but check the pack to make sure.

Lentil & okra curry

serves 4   prep time 15 minutes   cook time 40 minutes   freezable

A quick and easy vegan curry that's spiced up with fresh ginger and chilli.

Calorie controlled cooking spray

1 onion, finely chopped

2 garlic cloves, crushed

4cm piece fresh ginger, peeled and finely grated

1½ tablespoons curry powder

2 red chillies, 1 left whole and 1 sliced, to serve

150g dried red lentils, rinsed (see Cook's tip)

800ml vegetable stock, made with 2 stock cubes

350g okra, trimmed and cut into 3cm pieces

Small handful fresh coriander leaves, finely chopped, plus extra to serve

2 x 250g pouches microwave brown basmati rice

Lime wedges, to serve

1   Mist a large nonstick pan with cooking spray and set over a medium heat. Add the onion and cook for 6-8 minutes, until soft. Add the garlic, ginger, curry powder and the whole chilli and cook for another 2 minutes. Stir in the lentils and stock, then bring to a simmer. Cook, covered, for 20-25 minutes, stirring occasionally, until the lentils are tender.

2   Meanwhile, mist a large nonstick frying pan with cooking spray and set over a medium-high heat. Add the okra and cook for 5-6 minutes over a medium-high heat, until tender. Add the cooked okra and the coriander to the lentils. Remove and discard the chilli. Continue to cook uncovered for 5 minutes, until the sauce has reduced and thickened.

3   Prepare the rice to pack instructions, then divide between bowls. Top with the curry, scatter over the coriander and sliced chilli, and serve with the lime wedges.

The curry can be frozen in an airtight container for up to 2 months.

 SmartPoints value per serving

Cook's tip
To rinse the lentils, put them in a large sieve and hold under cold running water until the water runs clear.

Butternut squash mac & 'cheese'

serves 4   prep time 15 minutes   cook time 1 hour

Our vegan version of this family favourite looks and tastes amazing.

1 small butternut squash (about 1kg), peeled, deseeded and diced
Calorie controlled cooking spray
280g macaroni
2 tablespoons dairy-free spread
2 garlic cloves, crushed
2 tablespoons plain flour
½ tablespoon English mustard powder
450ml unsweetened almond milk
20g nutritional yeast
1 tablespoon snipped fresh chives, plus extra to serve
100g mixed salad leaves
Juice of ½ lemon

1   Preheat the oven to 200°C, fan 180°C, gas mark 6. Put the butternut squash into a roasting tin, mist with cooking spray, and season to taste. Roast for 35-40 minutes until tender and golden, then blitz in a food processor or mash until smooth.

2   Meanwhile, cook the pasta for 6-8 minutes until just al dente, then drain and set aside.

3   Put the spread into a large pan set over a medium-high heat. Once melted, add the garlic and cook for 1 minute. Add the flour and mustard powder and cook, stirring constantly, for 4-5 minutes.

4   Gradually stir in the almond milk and gently simmer for 10 minutes until the sauce is thick enough to coat the back of a spoon. Season to taste and stir in the nutritional yeast and mashed squash until well combined. Add the pasta and chives and stir to combine, then pour into a 1.2 litre baking dish and bake for 20 minutes until lightly golden.

5   Dress the salad leaves with the lemon juice, then serve with the macaroni cheese, with the extra chives scattered over.

 SmartPoints value per serving

Cook's tip
Top with some sliced tomatoes before baking, for no extra Smartpoints.

Pulled jackfruit burgers with celeriac fries

serves 4   prep time 10 minutes   cook time 45 minutes

Never tried jackfruit? These delicious burgers are a great way to start.

Calorie controlled cooking spray

1 small onion, thinly sliced

2 garlic cloves, crushed

1½ tablespoons smoked paprika

2 teaspoons ground cumin

400g tin chopped tomatoes

2 tablespoons barbecue sauce

1 teaspoon Tabasco sauce

**2 x 400g tins jackfruit
in water, drained**

**1kg celeriac, unpeeled, cut into
2cm thick chips**

1 tablespoon cornflour

½ tablespoon olive oil

**1 tablespoon finely chopped
fresh coriander**

**½ tablespoon finely chopped
fresh flat-leaf parsley**

4 x 60g white burger buns

**1 Little Gem lettuce,
leaves separated**

1 large tomato, sliced

4 tablespoons plain soya yogurt

1   Mist a large pan with cooking spray and set over a medium heat. Add the onion and cook for 6-8 minutes until soft, then add the garlic and spices and cook for another minute. Add the tomatoes, along with half a tin of water, the barbecue sauce, Tabasco sauce and jackfruit, and season to taste. Cover and gently simmer for 15 minutes, then remove the lid and simmer for another 20 minutes until the sauce has reduced and the jackfruit has started to break down. Roughly shred the jackfruit with two forks.

2   Meanwhile, preheat the oven to 220°C, fan 200°C, gas mark 7. Put the celeriac chips on a large baking sheet, toss with the cornflour and oil, and season to taste. Bake for 35 minutes, turning halfway through, until golden and tender, then toss with the coriander and parsley.

3   Split the buns and toast until golden, then top with the lettuce, tomato, jackfruit, soya yogurt and bun tops. Serve with the celeriac fries on the side.

   SmartPoints value per serving

Cook's tip
The pulled jackfruit will keep covered in the fridge for up to 2 days.

Snacks & desserts

92 Mini butternut & sage veggie rolls

94 Roasted broccoli houmous with crudités

96 Mushroom & thyme pasties

98 Tofu nuggets with ranch-style dressing

100 Summer rolls with satay sauce

102 Cacio e pepe chickpeas

104 Cacao & banana ice 'cream'

106 Lemon meringue tart

108 Vegan crème caramel

110 Chocolate celebration cake

Mini butternut & sage veggie rolls

makes 16   prep time 15 minutes + chilling   cook time 1 hour 5 minutes

Add one of these veggie rolls to your lunchbox for a delicious afternoon snack.

400g prepared butternut squash, diced

1 large onion, cut into small wedges

1 small garlic bulb, unpeeled

Calorie controlled cooking spray

12 fresh sage leaves, roughly torn

40g grated vegetarian Italian-style hard cheese

1 teaspoon chilli flakes

375g light ready-rolled puff pastry

1 egg, lightly beaten

2 tablespoons tomato ketchup

1   Preheat the oven to 200°C, fan 180°C, gas mark 6 and line a large baking tray with baking paper. Put the squash, onion and garlic into a large roasting tin, season to taste and mist with cooking spray. Roast for 35-40 minutes, turning and adding the sage halfway through.

2   Put the cooked squash, onion and sage into a food processor and squeeze in the garlic flesh when cool enough to handle. Add 30g of the cheese, season to taste and pulse to a rough purée, then stir in the chilli flakes and allow to cool completely.

3   Cut the pastry in half lengthways and spoon half of the mixture down the centre of each piece – it will be quite wet. Brush one edge of the pastry with a little of the beaten egg and fold it over the filling, trying not to let the filling escape. Seal the edges with a fork and cut each roll into 8 pieces. Put the rolls onto the prepared tray, brush the tops with beaten egg and scatter over the remaining cheese. Chill in the fridge for 15 minutes, then bake for 20-25 minutes until golden and risen, and serve with the tomato ketchup for dipping.

 SmartPoints value per roll

Cook's tip

To make these vegan, swap the cheese in the filling for 40g nutritional yeast and brush with 2 teaspoons melted dairy-free spread instead of egg, then top with 1 teaspoon nigella seeds instead of cheese, for the same SmartPoints.

Roasted broccoli houmous with crudités

serves 4   prep time 10 minutes   cook time 25 minutes

Roasted garlic and broccoli add loads of flavour and colour to this tasty houmous.

250g Tenderstem broccoli

2 small garlic cloves, unpeeled

Calorie controlled cooking spray

400g tin chickpeas, drained and rinsed

1 tablespoon tahini

1 tablespoon extra-virgin olive oil

1 teaspoon ground cumin

120g plain soya yogurt

Grated zest and juice of ½ lemon

100g baby heritage carrots

100g baby sweetcorn

50g chicory, leaves separated

2 celery sticks, cut into 5cm lengths

1 small cucumber, deseeded and cut into batons

1   Preheat the oven to 200°C, fan 180°C, gas mark 6. Put the broccoli and garlic into a large roasting tin, season to taste, then mist with cooking spray. Roast for 25 minutes until golden and tender. Roughly chop the broccoli and squeeze the garlic cloves from their skins, then set aside to cool.

2   Put the cooled broccoli and garlic into a food processor with the chickpeas, tahini, oil, cumin, yogurt, lemon zest and juice. Season to taste and blitz until smooth. Spoon into a serving bowl and serve with the vegetable crudités for dipping.

2   SmartPoints value per serving

Cook's tip
Use 0% fat Greek yogurt instead of soya yogurt if you aren't vegan. The houmous will keep in an airtight container in the fridge for up to 2 days.

Mushroom & thyme pasties

makes 12   **prep time** 20 minutes + chilling   **cook time** 40 minutes   **freezable**

These mini vegan pasties are perfect for family get-togethers and picnics.

Calorie controlled cooking spray

2 eschallion shallots, finely chopped

500g chestnut mushrooms, roughly chopped

3 garlic cloves, finely chopped

5 large sprigs fresh thyme, leaves stripped and roughly chopped

70ml white wine (vegan friendly)

1 tablespoon finely chopped fresh flat-leaf parsley

2 x 375g packs light, vegan ready-rolled shortcrust pastry (675g used)

2 tablespoons unsweetened almond milk

1   Preheat the oven to 200°C, fan 180°C fan, gas mark 6 and line a large baking tray with baking paper.

2   Mist a large nonstick frying pan with cooking spray and set over a medium-high heat. Add the shallots and cook for 6-7 minutes until soft, then add the mushrooms and cook for another 3-4 minutes until soft. Stir in the garlic and thyme and cook for another minute, then pour in the wine and simmer for 3-4 minutes until the liquid has evaporated. Season to taste and stir in the parsley, then set aside to cool completely.

3   Cut each sheet of pastry into six squares. Divide the mushroom mixture into 12, then put a portion onto the centre of each square, leaving a 2cm border. Brush the borders with water and fold in half to make triangles. Trim the points of the triangles into semi-circles and discard the excess pastry. Crimp the edges and repeat with the remaining pasties, then put the pasties on the prepared baking tray with the crimped edge at the top and chill in the fridge for 15 minutes.

4   Brush the pasties with the almond milk, then bake for 25 minutes until golden, then cool for 10 minutes before serving.

 7   **SmartPoints value per pasty**

Cook's tip

Keep the pasties in an airtight container in the fridge for up to 2 days and reheat in a low oven until piping hot.

Tofu nuggets with ranch-style dressing

serves 4 **prep time** 25 minutes **cook time** 10 minutes

Cubes of tofu are fried in crisp breadcrumbs and served with a delicious dipping sauce.

280g block extra-firm tofu

75ml unsweetened almond milk

2 tablespoons plain flour

75g panko breadcrumbs

½ teaspoon sweet smoked paprika

¼ teaspoon mild chilli powder

¼ teaspoon ground turmeric

½ teaspoon garlic granules

200g plain soya yogurt

1 tablespoon cider vinegar

2 teaspoons maple syrup

Juice of ½ lemon, plus lemon wedges, to serve

½ tablespoon finely chopped fresh dill, plus extra, to serve

½ tablespoon snipped fresh chives, plus extra, to serve

Calorie controlled cooking spray

1 Drain the tofu, then wrap it in kitchen paper and place between two plates. Weigh down the top plate with a tin and set aside for 15 minutes, then cut the tofu into 3cm cubes.

2 Put the almond milk and flour in a small bowl and whisk until you have a smooth batter. Put the breadcrumbs, paprika, chilli powder, turmeric and garlic granules in another bowl and stir to combine. Dip the tofu cubes into the batter to coat, then roll in the breadcrumb mixture and set aside.

3 Whisk the yogurt, vinegar, maple syrup and lemon juice together in a small bowl and stir in the herbs.

4 Mist a large nonstick frying pan set over a medium-high heat with cooking spray and fry the nuggets for 3-4 minutes, until golden on all sides. You may need to do this in batches. Serve with the dipping sauce and an extra scattering of herbs, with the lemon wedges to squeeze over.

3 **SmartPoints value per serving**

Cook's tip
Use any unsweetened dairy-free milk, or replace soya yogurt with fat-free natural yogurt, if you prefer.

Summer rolls with satay sauce

makes 8   prep time **20 minutes**   cook time **3 minutes**

These tasty Vietnamese-inspired snacks couldn't be simpler to make.

75g rice vermicelli noodles

**8 Vietnamese rice
paper wrappers**

**1 large carrot, cut
into matchsticks**

**1 small cucumber, cut
into matchsticks**

**1 orange or yellow pepper,
deseeded and cut into thin slices**

**2 spring onions, trimmed and
thickly sliced**

**Large handful fresh
coriander leaves**

1 tablespoon vegetable oil

½ tablespoon rice vinegar

Juice of 1½ limes

**1 small red chilli, deseeded and
finely chopped**

2 tablespoons PBfit

½ tablespoons light soy sauce

2 teaspoons agave syrup

1   Cook the noodles to pack instructions, then cool under cold running water and drain.

2   Carefully fill a shallow bowl with hot water and dip a wrapper into the water until pliable. Transfer the wrapper to a board and place one-eighth of the noodles, vegetables and coriander in a line on one side of the wrapper, leaving a 3cm border at the top and bottom.

3   Mix the oil, rice vinegar, one-third of the lime juice and the chilli together, then spoon a little over the vegetables. Fold the top and bottom of the wrapper over the ends of the vegetables, then roll the vegetables up in the wrapper and set aside. Repeat with the remaining wrappers.

4   In a small bowl, mix the PBfit with 1½ tablespoons cold water, soy sauce, agave syrup and remaining lime juice, and serve alongside the rolls for dipping.

3   SmartPoints value per roll

Cook's tip
Leave the chilli out if
you don't like spice.

Cacio e pepe chickpeas

serves 4   **prep time 5 minutes**   **cook time 35 minutes**

For a great alternative to crisps or nuts, try these delicious nibbles.

2 x 400g tins chickpeas, drained and rinsed

1 tablespoon olive oil

1 teaspoon coarsely ground black pepper

30g grated vegetarian Italian-style hard cheese

1   Preheat the oven to 200°C, fan 180°C, gas mark 6. Pat the chickpeas dry with kitchen paper and put into a large bowl. Toss the chickpeas with the oil, pepper and 20g of the cheese, then spread them out on a large baking tray.

2   Bake for 30-35 minutes, shaking the tray halfway though, until the chickpeas are crisp and golden. Allow to cool completely, then serve with the remaining grated cheese scattered over.

2 **SmartPoints value per serving**

Cook's tip
Make sure you dry the chickpeas thoroughly before roasting as it helps them to become crisp. The roasted chickpeas will keep in an airtight container for up to 2 days.

Cacao & banana ice 'cream'

serves 4   prep time 5 minutes + freezing

This easy, 3-ingredient dessert is full of rich, chocolatey flavour.

4 ripe bananas, roughly chopped
3 tablespoons cacao powder
1 tablespoon pistachio kernels, finely chopped

1 Put the chopped bananas in a freezerproof food bag, seal and freeze for at least 4 hours, or overnight.

2 Put the frozen bananas and the cacao powder into the bowl of a small food processor or blender and blitz until smooth.

3 Serve immediately with the pistachios scattered over, or transfer to a freezerproof container and freeze until ready to serve.

The dessert can be frozen in an airtight container for up to 2 months.

 SmartPoints value per serving

Cook's tip
You could use either cacao or cocoa powder in this recipe. Cacao is made from raw cacao beans, while cocoa is made from roasted cacao. Both may contain other ingredients that are not vegan. Always check the labels to make sure.

Lemon meringue tart

serves 12   prep time 30 minutes + chilling   cook time 40 minutes

The meringue on top of this vegan tart is made from a surprising ingredient.

375g light, vegan ready-rolled shortcrust pastry (115g used)

Grated zest and juice of 5 large lemons, plus extra grated zest to serve (you'll need about 200ml juice)

225g caster sugar

4½ tablespoons cornflour

40g dairy-free spread

100g plain soya yogurt

Liquid from a 400g tin chickpeas (you'll need 80ml), chilled

1   Preheat the oven to 190°C, fan 170°C, gas mark 5. Line a 20cm loose-bottomed fluted tart tin with the pastry, then trim and discard the excess. Prick the pastry all over with a fork, then line with baking paper and fill with baking beans. Bake for 15 minutes until just golden, then remove the beans and paper and bake for another 5-10 minutes. Remove from the oven and let cool completely in the tin.

2   Meanwhile, make the curd. Put the lemon zest, juice and 150g sugar into a small pan set over a medium heat. Heat, stirring, until the sugar has dissolved. Put the cornflour in a small bowl and whisk in a tablespoon of water to make a paste, then add the paste to the pan. Whisk for 1-2 minutes until very thick, then stir in the spread and soya yogurt until combined. Transfer to a bowl, cover with clingfilm and allow to cool completely. Once cool, spoon the curd into the cooked pastry case and chill in the fridge for 1 hour.

3   Heat the grill to medium-high. Put the chickpea liquid into a large bowl and whisk with a hand-held electric whisk for 10 minutes until stiff peaks form. Add the remaining sugar, 2 tablespoons at a time, whisking each time until dissolved. Spoon the meringue over the lemon curd and put under the grill for 1-2 minutes until lightly browned (or use a kitchen blowtorch). Scatter over the extra lemon zest, then serve.

7   **SmartPoints value per serving**

Cook's tip
The assembled tart is best served the day it's made, but you can make the pastry case and lemon curd up to 2 days in advance. Keep the pastry case in an airtight container at room temperature and the curd in the fridge.

Vegan crème caramel

makes 6   **prep time 10 minutes + chilling**   **cook time 10 minutes**

The classic dessert is reinvented using almond milk and tofu.

75g caster sugar
2 x 349g packs firm silken tofu
100ml unsweetened almond milk
6 tablespoons maple syrup
4 tablespoons cornflour
1 tablespoon vanilla bean paste

1 Put the caster sugar in a small dry frying pan set over a medium-high heat. Cook for 8-10 minutes, swirling the pan (not stirring), until the sugar melts into a light-brown caramel. Remove from the heat. Carefully divide the caramel between 6 x 180ml ramekins, then set aside.

2 Put the tofu, almond milk, maple syrup, cornflour and vanilla bean paste into a small food processor or blender and blitz until completely smooth.

3 Transfer the tofu mixture to a pan and set over a medium heat. Cook for 5 minutes, whisking continuously, until thickened – it should be the consistency of a thick yogurt.

4 Remove from the heat and divide the mixture between the ramekins, pouring it over the caramel. Transfer to the fridge and chill for 3 hours or until set.

5 Briefly dip the base of each ramekin into a pan of just-boiled water to loosen the edges of the crème caramels. Carefully turn out onto plates to serve.

8   SmartPoints value per crème caramel

Cook's tip
The caramel will set firmly in the ramekins and chilling them helps it form a thin, liquid sauce, so it's best to make these at the start of the day to enjoy for dessert later.

Chocolate celebration cake

serves 14   **prep time** 20 minutes + cooling   **cook time** 25 minutes   **freezable**

This showstopping vegan cake is perfect for a birthday or family celebration.

**270g dairy-free spread, plus
1 teaspoon for greasing**

150g caster sugar

280g self-raising flour

9 tablespoons cacao powder

1 teaspoon baking powder

1 teaspoon bicarbonate of soda

280ml unsweetened almond milk

1 tablespoon white wine vinegar

3 tablespoons icing sugar

**150g strawberries, hulled and
sliced, plus a few extra whole
strawberries to decorate**

150g raspberries

1   Preheat the oven to 190°C, fan 170°C, gas mark 5. Grease
2 x 18cm sandwich tins with low-fat spread and line the bases
and sides with baking paper. Put 150g of the spread and all
the caster sugar into a large bowl and beat with a hand-held
electric whisk for 4-5 minutes, until light and fluffy.

2   In another large bowl, combine the flour, 6 tablespoons of
the cacao powder, the baking powder and bicarbonate of soda.
Whisk half of the dry ingredients into the spread and sugar
mixture using the hand-held electric whisk. In a large jug,
combine the almond milk and vinegar, then whisk half of this
into the cake mixture. Repeat with the remaining dry ingredients
and almond milk mixture until you have a smooth batter.

3   Divide the batter between the prepared tins and smooth the
surfaces with a spatula. Bake for 25 minutes, or until a skewer
inserted into the centre of the cakes comes out clean. Set aside
to cool in the tins for 15 minutes, then carefully release from the
tins and transfer to a wire rack to cool completely.

4   Put the remaining spread in a medium bowl and sift over
2½ tablespoons of the cacao powder and all the icing sugar.
Whisk to combine.

5   Put one of the sponges on a cake stand and top with the
'buttercream', most of the sliced strawberries, half of the
raspberries, and the second sponge. Sift over the remaining
cacao powder, then serve decorated with the remaining
strawberries and raspberries.

The unfilled sponge can be frozen, tightly wrapped in clingfilm
and then kitchen foil, for up to 2 months.

Cook's tip
The cake will keep in an
airtight container in the
fridge for up to 3-4 days.

10   SmartPoints value per serving

Recipe index

APPLES
Cherry Bakewell Bircher muesli   20
Apricot & pistachio breakfast bars   32
ARTICHOKES
Olive & artichoke tart   64
ASPARAGUS
Green goddess egg muffins   44
Primavera orzo pasta salad   40
AUBERGINES
Griddled aubergine bánh mì   36
Smoky aubergine chilli with
cauliflower 'rice'   72
AVOCADO
Breakfast burrito   22
Moroccan-style avocado on toast   18

BANANAS
Apricot & pistachio breakfast bars   32
Cacao & banana ice 'cream'   104
Oat waffles with mixed berries   24
BEANS
Breakfast burrito   22
Butter bean pancakes with fresh
strawberries   14
Halloumi curry   66
Hash brown traybake   28
Smoky aubergine chilli with
cauliflower 'rice'   72
Smoky borlotti bean soup   52
Vegan fry-up   16
Veggie sushi bowl   56
BEETROOT
Beetroot & feta filo galette   82
Beetroot falafel pittas   50
BERRIES
Butter bean pancakes with fresh
strawberries   14
Chocolate celebration cake   110
Oat waffles with mixed berries   24
Bombay potato frittata   38
BREAD
Beetroot falafel pittas   50
Caprese panini rolls   46
Coronation chickpea open
sandwich   54
Griddled aubergine bánh mì   36
Herby scrambled tofu with
griddled tomatoes   30
Menemen   26
Moroccan-style avocado on toast   18
Pulled jackfruit burgers with
celeriac fries   88
Roasted chickpea gyros   58
Vegan fry-up   16
Breakfast burrito   22
BROCCOLI
Cheese & onion pie with
minted greens   76

Green goddess egg muffins   44
Primavera orzo pasta salad   40
Roasted broccoli houmous
with crudités   94
Butter bean pancakes with fresh
strawberries   14
BUTTERNUT SQUASH
Butternut squash mac & 'cheese'   86
Mini butternut & sage veggie rolls   92
Tahini butternut couscous bowl   48

CABBAGE
Griddled aubergine bánh mì   36
Smoky borlotti bean soup   52
Cacao & banana ice 'cream'   104
Cacio e pepe chickpeas   102
CAKE
Chocolate celebration cake   110
Caprese panini rolls   46
CAULIFLOWER
Moroccan-style cauliflower soup   60
Smoky aubergine chilli with
cauliflower 'rice'   72
Sweet & sour cauliflower with rice   78
CELERIAC
Pulled jackfruit burgers with
celeriac fries   88
CELERY
Roasted broccoli houmous
with crudités   94
Smoky borlotti bean soup   52
CHEESE
Beetroot & feta filo galette   82
Breakfast burrito   22
Cacio e pepe chickpeas   102
Cheese & onion pie with
minted greens   76
Halloumi curry   66
Hash brown traybake   28
Mini butternut & sage veggie rolls   92
Olive & artichoke tart   64
Romesco-style pasta bake   68
Cherry Bakewell Bircher muesli   20
CHICKPEAS
Beetroot falafel pittas   50
Cacio e pepe chickpeas   102
Coronation chickpea open
sandwich   54
Halloumi curry   66
Roasted broccoli houmous
with crudités   94
Roasted chickpea gyros   58
Sweetcorn & carrot fritters   70
CHICORY
Roasted broccoli houmous
with crudités   94
CHOCOLATE
Cacao & banana ice 'cream'   104

Chocolate celebration cake   110
Coronation chickpea open sandwich   54
COURGETTES
Green tagine with preserved
lemon couscous   80
Hash brown traybake   28
COUSCOUS
Green tagine with preserved
lemon couscous   80
Tahini butternut couscous bowl   48
CUCUMBER
Beetroot falafel pittas   50
Green goddess egg muffins   44
Roasted broccoli houmous
with crudités   94
Roasted chickpea gyros   58
Summer rolls with satay sauce   100
Veggie sushi bowl   56
CURRY
Bombay potato frittata   38
Halloumi curry   66
Lentil & okra curry   84

EGGS
Bombay potato frittata   38
Breakfast burrito   22
Cheese & onion pie with
minted greens   76
Green goddess egg muffins   44
Hash brown traybake   28
Menemen   26
Mini butternut & sage veggie rolls   92
Olive & artichoke tart   64
Sweetcorn & carrot fritters   70

FENNEL
Green tagine with preserved
lemon couscous   80

Green goddess egg muffins   44
Green tagine with preserved lemon
couscous   80
Griddled aubergine bánh mì   36

Halloumi curry   66
Hash brown traybake   28
Herby scrambled tofu with
griddled tomatoes   30
HOUMOUS
Beetroot falafel pittas   50
Roasted broccoli houmous
with crudités   94

JACKFRUIT
Pulled jackfruit burgers with
celeriac fries   88

Kale, mango & cashew salad   42

LEEKS
Primavera orzo
pasta salad   40
Lemon meringue tart   106

LENTILS
Beetroot & feta filo galette   82
Lentil & okra curry   84

MANGOS
Kale, mango & cashew salad   42
Menemen   26
Mini butternut & sage veggie rolls   92
Moroccan-style avocado on toast   18
Moroccan-style cauliflower soup   60

MUFFINS
Green goddess egg muffins   44

MUSHROOMS
Hash brown traybake   28
Mushroom & thyme pasties   96
Vegan fry-up   16

NOODLES
Summer rolls with satay sauce   100

OATS
Apricot & pistachio breakfast bars   32
Cherry Bakewell Bircher muesli   20
Oat waffles with mixed berries   24

OKRA
Lentil & okra curry   84

OLIVES
Green tagine with preserved
lemon couscous   80
Olive & artichoke tart   64

PANCAKES
Butter bean pancakes with fresh
strawberries   14

PASTA
Butternut squash mac & 'cheese'   86
Primavera orzo pasta salad   40
Romesco-style pasta bake   68
Sun-dried tomato carbonara   74

PASTRY
Beetroot & feta filo galette   82
Cheese & onion pie with
minted greens   76
Lemon meringue tart   106
Mini butternut & sage veggie rolls   92
Mushroom & thyme pasties   96
Olive & artichoke tart   64

PEAS
Cheese & onion pie with
minted greens   76
Primavera orzo pasta salad   40

PEPPERS
Breakfast burrito   22

Menemen   26
Romesco-style pasta bake   68
Summer rolls with satay sauce   100
Sweet & sour cauliflower with rice   78
Tahini butternut couscous bowl   48
Veggie sushi bowl   56

PESTO
Primavera orzo pasta salad   40

PIES
Cheese & onion pie with
minted greens   76

PINEAPPLE
Sweet & sour cauliflower with rice   78

POTATOES
Bombay potato frittata   38
Cheese & onion pie with
minted greens   76
Hash brown traybake   28
Primavera orzo pasta salad   40
Pulled jackfruit burgers with
celeriac fries   88

RICE
Halloumi curry   66
Lentil & okra curry   84
Sweet & sour cauliflower with rice   78
Veggie sushi bowl   56
Roasted broccoli houmous
with crudités   94
Roasted chickpea gyros   58
Romesco-style pasta bake   68

SALAD
Green goddess egg muffins   44
Kale, mango & cashew salad   42
Primavera orzo pasta salad   40
Smoky aubergine chilli with
cauliflower 'rice'   72
Smoky borlotti bean soup   52

SOUP
Moroccan-style cauliflower soup   60
Smoky borlotti bean soup   52

SOYA YOGURT
Kale, mango & cashew salad   42
Lemon meringue tart   106
Oat waffles with mixed berries   24
Pulled jackfruit burgers with
celeriac fries   88
Roasted broccoli houmous
with crudités   94
Smoky aubergine chilli with
cauliflower 'rice'   72

Smoky borlotti
bean soup   52
Tofu nuggets with
ranch-style dressing   98
Summer rolls with satay sauce   100

SUN-DRIED TOMATOES
Sun-dried tomato carbonara   74
Tahini butternut couscous bowl   48
Sweet & sour cauliflower with rice   78

SWEETCORN
Roasted broccoli houmous
with crudités   94
Sweetcorn & carrot fritters   70

TAHINI
Roasted broccoli houmous
with crudités   94
Tahini butternut couscous bowl   48

TOFU
Caprese panini rolls   46
Herby scrambled tofu with
griddled tomatoes   30
Tofu nuggets with ranch-style
dressing   98
Vegan crème caramel   108

TORTILLA CHIPS
Smoky aubergine chilli with
cauliflower 'rice'   72

Vegan crème caramel   108
Vegan fry-up   16
Veggie sushi bowl   56

WAFFLES
Oat waffles with mixed berries   24

YOGURT
Beetroot falafel pittas   50
Butter bean pancakes with fresh
strawberries   14
Coronation chickpea open sandwich   54
Halloumi curry   66
Moroccan-style cauliflower soup   60
Roasted chickpea gyros   58
Sweetcorn & carrot fritters   70

SmartPoints index

0 SmartPoints	Page	Serves
Smoky borlotti bean soup	52	4

1 SmartPoint

	Page	Serves
Smoky aubergine chilli with cauliflower 'rice'	72	4

2 SmartPoints

	Page	Serves
Cacao & banana ice 'cream'	104	4
Cacio e pepe chickpeas	102	4
Green goddess egg muffins	44	4
Roasted broccoli houmous with crudités	94	4
Sweetcorn & carrot fritters	70	4

3 SmartPoints

	Page	Serves
Mini butternut & sage veggie rolls	92	16
Moroccan-style cauliflower soup	60	4
Summer rolls with satay sauce	100	8
Tofu nuggets with ranch-style dressing	98	4

4 SmartPoints

	Page	Serves
Menemen	26	4
Vegan fry-up	16	4

5 SmartPoints

	Page	Serves
Apricot & pistachio breakfast bars	32	16
Herby scrambled tofu with griddled tomatoes	30	4
Kale, mango & cashew salad	42	4

6 SmartPoints

	Page	Serves
Butter bean pancakes with fresh strawberries	14	4
Coronation chickpea open sandwich	54	4
Green tagine with preserved lemon couscous	80	4
Hash brown traybake	28	6
Lentil & okra curry	84	4
Moroccan-style avocado on toast	18	4
Oat waffles with mixed berries	24	2
Pulled jackfruit burgers with celeriac fries	88	4

7 SmartPoints	Page	Serves
Beetroot & feta filo galette	82	4
Bombay potato frittata	38	4
Breakfast burrito	22	4
Cherry Bakewell Bircher muesli	20	4
Griddled aubergine bánh mì	36	4
Lemon meringue tart	106	12
Mushroom & thyme pasties	96	12
Olive & artichoke tart	64	6
Roasted chickpea gyros	58	4

8 SmartPoints

	Page	Serves
Sweet & sour cauliflower with rice	78	4
Tahini butternut couscous bowl	48	4
Vegan crème caramel	108	6
Veggie sushi bowl	56	4

10 SmartPoints

	Page	Serves
Beetroot falafel pittas	50	4
Butternut squash mac & 'cheese'	86	4
Chocolate celebration cake	110	14
Romesco-style pasta bake	68	4

11 SmartPoints

	Page	Serves
Primavera orzo pasta salad	40	4

12 SmartPoints

	Page	Serves
Caprese panini rolls	46	4
Cheese & onion pie with minted greens	76	4
Halloumi curry	66	4

14 SmartPoints

	Page	Serves
Sun-dried tomato carbonara	74	4